D0443355

Everyday
Commitments

Everyday Commitments

~❧

Choosing a Life of Love,
Realism, and Acceptance

David Richo

SHAMBHALA
Boston & London
2008

SHAMBHALA PUBLICATIONS, INC.
Horticultural Hall
300 Massachusetts Avenue
Boston, Massachusetts 02115
www.shambhala.com

9 8 7 6 5 4 3 2 1

First Edition

Printed in the United States of America

♾ This edition is printed on acid-free paper that meets the
American National Standards Institute z39.48 Standard.
Distributed in the United States by Random House, Inc.,
and in Canada by Random House of Canada Ltd

Designed by Jeff Baker

Library of Congress Cataloging-in-Publication Data

Richo, David, 1940–
Everyday commitments: choosing a life of love, realism,
and acceptance / David Richo.—1st ed.
p. cm.
ISBN 978-1-59030-562-1 (hardcover: alk. paper)
1. Life. 2. Attitude (Psychology) 3. Success. 4. Spirituality.
I. Title.
BD431.R525 2008
170'.44—dc22
2007024643

To each of my students and clients
throughout the years,
with love, respect, and thanks.

So much of what I know
I learned from you.
We all have let the light
Come in and through.

Contents

Introduction

To be human is to be born into the world
with something to achieve, namely, the
fullness of one's human nature.

—Paul Wadell, CP

Life is a challenging journey. Although we hope that our lives will be easy, comfortable, and serene, they are often complicated, conflicted, and disappointing. Too many of us bear the scars of painful experiences, suffer from low self-esteem, and become trapped in cycles of self-destructive behavior. And so the happiness we desire often eludes us.

To set our lives on a positive course, we can begin developing loving-kindness toward ourselves and others. When we learn to approach ourselves with friendliness and caring, the dynamics of our lives begin to shift. In the Buddhist tradition, and in many other religious traditions, this is a primary pathway to happiness and spiritual growth.

In this book I offer fifty-two commitments that help us grow in self-respect and loving-kindness. This enterprise involves saying yes to three things: We say yes to the basic goodness in all of us and in all the universe. We say yes to who we are and who others are, not just once but in all our daily behaviors. Finally, we say yes to reality as it is. The art of acceptance forms the foundation of our own integrity and our healthy love of ourselves and others.

The commitments are a catalog of human strengths and abilities. They can also be called virtues, in the sense that they are habits of wholesomeness and love. Virtues are the building blocks of self-respect, integrity, and compassion. We might say virtuous living is proper spiritual etiquette in a world of greed, hate, and delusion. Our new definition of success is not in what we have gained nor in how we "had it our way." Our success is in how we acted honestly, lovingly, and realistically.

We begin by taking small steps, outlined in the paragraphs that follow each commitment. Soon we find that we are acting wholesomely and lovingly without having to put so much effort or thought into it. The Roman philosopher Seneca noticed this result: "My goodness now requires no thought but has become habit and I cannot act but rightly."

The commitments and exercises offered in this book are not strategies by which we seek to gain perfection or happiness, in the conventional senses of those words. The purpose of the commitments is to help us live our lives at a heart level. Our destiny is to display in our lifetime the timeless design of love and wholeness that has always been inside us. Choices and attitudes that show integrity and loving-kindness help us do that. They locate and display the intrinsic, basic goodness we all possess, which was referred to by Seneca, by the Buddha, and by many other spiritual teachers.

Taken together, the commitments in this book offer a depiction of our basic goodness, and they offer specific ways to articulate our inherent kindness and compassion in daily life. The exercises and practices combine the goals of helping ourselves and helping others. Changing our personal standards in the ways described here will help us and will also help the people we interact with. When we grow in loving-kindness, everyone benefits.

According to a recent article in the *Washington Post*, scientists are discovering that our moral sense may be "hardwired" in us, residing in an area of the brain called the ventromedial prefrontal cortex.* Marc Hauser, a professor of psychology and evolutionary biology at Harvard, agrees that morality may be intrinsic to humans rather than the result of religious or cultural teachings. This suggests that when we act morally, we align ourselves with our own biology and with the natural world. Empathy is the foundation of our moral inclinations, and science is beginning to demonstrate that loving-kindness, rather than being a precept handed down to us from

---

* Shankar Vedantam, "If It Feels Good to Be Good, It Might Be Only Natural," *Washington Post*, May 28, 2007.

above, flows from within. Perhaps this is why the teaching of inherent goodness came into being in so many spiritual traditions.

The commitments that follow may be inspiring but also intimidating. Very few of us can achieve all of these ideals to the fullest. Nonetheless, we can set our bar high, and then make some strides and perhaps some leaps. Any advance frees us from fear-based living in favor of healthy love for ourselves and others.

We will feel the results not only in increased self-esteem and a deeper acceptance of reality, but in our bodies: We take our rightful space in the world. We feel a warmth coming through us, making touch and closeness easier to show. We feel our hearts open in a universally embracing and, yes, sometimes aching, way. Virginia Woolf expressed it best in her novel *The Waves:* "Things are losing their hardness. Even my body now lets the light through."

How to Use This Book

This book offers fifty-two commitments presented in the form of short, concise chapters. Each chapter opens with the commitment itself, followed by a short commentary that includes a practical exercise. The commitments are not meant to be "shoulds" or moral directives, but gentle invitations that stir and steer us to new possibilities in our way of being in the world. They are challenges, guidelines, and opportunities, not demands or obligations. The commitments can be used as firm dedications to grow and change. They can also be used as aspirations, intentions, or affirmations that get us started in making changes in ourselves and in our way of being with others. They also offer a means of self-exploration and self-assessment: To what extent does sanity and love characterize my present behavior and attitudes?

Ultimately, the commitments presented here are paths to *contentment* with ourselves as we are and can be, and with the world as it is and may be.

Here are some specific suggestions about ways to work with this book:

- Before contemplating a commitment, take a few deep breaths and notice how you feel physically. Slowing ourselves down in this way and opening ourselves to the moment can help us to benefit from the new ideas and directions presented in this book. Before trying any of the exercises or practices described in the commentary, also make a habit of stopping to take a few deep breaths and notice any bodily sensations.
- Ponder one commitment (and the commentary that follows it) each day or one each week and look for ways to design your behavior accordingly.

- Read aloud (or transcribe) one commitment each day or one commitment each week.
- Record yourself reading each commitment aloud (onto a tape or voice recorder) and listen to them from time to time. Hearing yourself stating the commitments reinforces them as guidelines in your daily life.
- Use the statements for reflecting on the ethical choices you have faced in the past and that might be facing you now. Look upon your past decisions with compassionate understanding and without regret or self-blame. Commit yourself to healthy actions for the future.
- Look for practical and specific ways to implement these ideals. In the commentary that follows each commitment, you will find some leads for this, but the ones you think of are usually best.
- Practices gain power as we listen to messages from our unconscious. Open up to this possibility by freely and spontaneously writing a poem or journal entry in response to a commitment. Pay closer attention to dreams and synchronicity (meaningful coincidence) to see if they reflect themes that are similar to those in the practices you are engaging with.
- Use the statements as a self-assessment tool: Which commitments come easily? Which do not? Where are you progressing? Where do you feel

blocked? Ask someone you love and trust to give you feedback on how you reflect—or do not yet fully reflect—these ideals.

- Consider whether the commitments might work for you as a list of qualifications for a lifetime partner.

The key to spiritual maturation is transforming all of life, adversity included, into spiritual practice.

—B. Alan Wallace, *Buddhism with an Attitude*

The Commitments

1 Cultivating Loving-Kindness

❧ I am always looking for ways to intend,
express, and act with loving-kindness.

According to the Buddhist tradition, our inherent goodness is comprised of four qualities: loving-kindness, compassion, joy, and equanimity. This is our nature, yet we
often find ourselves drifting off course. The loving-kindness meditation practice helps us to cultivate these gifts
for ourselves and others. Find a place where you can sit
quietly, free of distractions, and follow these steps:

Begin with a few minutes of silence, taking deep
breaths and noticing any feelings or bodily sensations.
Say aloud, "May I experience loving-kindness," continuing for as long as feels comfortable. Then extend the same
quality to someone you love, saying: "May [name a person you love] experience loving-kindness." Next, extend
it to someone you feel indifferent toward, then to someone you're having difficulties with, then finally to all beings. The cycle can then be repeated, focusing on compassion, joy, and equanimity, one at a time. When we do
this practice, our circle of love is complete, all-inclusive,

and unconditional. We can repeat this practice each day or in any circumstance that seems to call for it. We can also alter the phrases we use, as long as we express heartfelt care for ourselves and others. This practice can help us let go of ego as we apply it in situations that might ordinarily arouse our aggression. For instance, when someone cuts us off in traffic, we can take a breath, slow down, and say aloud: "May you arrive safely at your destination without harming anyone. May you find serenity in courteous driving. May you become enlightened."

2   *Saying Yes to Reality*

❧ More and more, I say yes to the givens of human life: Everything changes and ends; things will not always go according to plan; life is not always fair or pain-free; and people are not always loving, honest, generous, or loyal.

This practice is simple and profound: cultivating an attitude of yes, a commitment to accept the things over which we have no control, without protest or blame. Yes is a choice to honor reality just as it is. It is not resigning ourselves but reconciling ourselves to reality, that is, aligning ourselves to it. Such freedom from illusion and wishful thinking is a form of enlightenment. We do all we can to change things that can be changed and then we accept what cannot be changed. We no longer attempt to control how others may act but allow them to be who they are and to make the choices they make. In facing life predicaments, we let the chips fall where they may and then do our best to play them to the best benefit of ourselves and others. When we receive the news that we have not been chosen for a job we feel disappointed. Yet that does not stop us from continuing our job search. We are at least now more adept at interviewing skills thanks to our recent try. As we practice the unconditional yes we notice that we no longer ask: "Why?" or "Why me?" Now we simply say: "Yes, now what?" Then the things that happen to us reveal themselves to be the necessary ingredients of our personal evolution, the factors that make us people of depth, character, and compassion.

We express our feelings without blame or aggression and the charge around them dissipates. Saying yes to life as it is doesn't mean that we never feel disappointed or saddened by our lives. Saying yes means that whatever happens, we take the stance of remaining open and friendly toward our experience.

3 *Grounded, Not Swayed*

> ⤳ No matter what happens to me, I am in-
> tent on remaining personally grounded: no
> longer thrown off course by events or by
> my reactions to them.

We can trust that we already have some skills in handling
the daily trials, challenges, and agonies of life without
becoming destabilized. We do this when we let ourselves
go through an experience without being driven or
stopped by our fears or by our desires for a specific out-
come. Here are practical ways to do this: We remind ourselves that we have faced hurdles before with success and
this one is no different. We rally our support system, a
group of friends, a therapist, and any guides who stand by
us and help keep us on track. We ask them to call us on
our vagaries and awaken us if we drift off course. We seek
help from a power beyond our ego, in whatever form or
tradition that fits for us. To do all this may take work on
ourselves from self-help or therapeutic sources. We are
looking for ways to do this work.

4 Remaining Secure

~≈ The painful events in life have an impact
on me but they no longer impinge on my
serenity. I look for ways to remain secure
within myself and, at the same time, keep
trusting that I can handle what happens
and it can help me grow.

Being more spiritually conscious does not mean that the
behavior of others or the events of life do not get to us.
We feel the thud of all that happens to us, but we are not
thrown for a loop because of it. What are the ways we remain secure within ourselves and handle what happens?
We let ourselves feel the feelings that are appropriate to
the events without becoming stuck in them or bitter because of them. We freeze-frame when feelings hit us and
we imagine them flowing safely through our bodies, from
head to toe, and then going into the ground. We grow in
self-esteem as we notice that we can feel anything and
still come back to our own center thereafter. As a result,
we view our feelings as *valuable* rather than negative,
shameful, or unfortunate. As feelings are expressed and

resolved, we are left with no resentment about what triggered them. We then can more easily believe in how life unfolds in favor of our growth when we say yes to its knocks.

5   *Committed to the Work*

~≈ I am not perfect, but I am sincerely
   committed to working on myself.

Our goal is not perfection, only commitment to ongoing
work on ourselves. This work can be done in therapy and
through self-help tools such as assertiveness training,
support groups, bodywork, affirmations, stress reduction
techniques, and so on. The work is that of addressing,
processing, and resolving issues that remain unfinished
from our past or are stressful in the present. The work
pivots around themes like these:

- We explore our childhood and recognize how it
  now impacts our adult relationships and our self-
  confidence.
- We look at our fears, addictions, self-criticism, and
  obsessions. We notice whether we are comfortable
  with feelings. We consider whether guilt or shame
  inhibit us.
- We look at our ego with its need to control others
  or to act from a sense of entitlement to special
  treatment.

- We ask ourselves if we are assertive rather than passive or aggressive in our relationships with others.
- We look at our intimate relationships to see how contented, fearless, and loving they are.

After *addressing* these five areas we *process* what comes up from each of them. We do this by feeling fully whatever they arouse in us. We pay attention to how they hook up to past events and relationships. We notice if we have built defenses against knowing about all this. This attentiveness to our own story leads us to *resolve* the issues that have made it so dramatic or inhibiting. As a result, we can *restructure* our lives in ways that raise our self-esteem and make us more compassionate toward others. Our psychological work is balanced by our growth in spiritual consciousness, which is precisely the theme of the commitments and practices in this book.

6 Freedom from the Grip of Fear

≈≈ I accept the fact of fear, allow myself to feel
my fear fully, and act so that fear does not
interfere with my life choices.

We all feel afraid sometimes. This is an appropriate feeling and can be a signal of real danger or threat. At the
same time, we sometimes feel afraid without reason. Our
guesses and fantasies about what might happen keep us
afraid of events and experiences that may never befall us.
It is useless to attempt to eliminate fear altogether,
whether it be realistic or imagined. But there is one thing
we can prevent: We do not have to act on our fears. Here
is the "Triple A" practice: Admit, Allow, and Act. We
admit to ourselves and to someone we trust that we are
scared, rather than deny it or call it by another name, for
example, cold feet, discomfort, worry, uneasiness, nerv-
ousness, and so on. We *allow* ourselves to feel the fear
fully rather than try to avoid it or drown it out with drugs
or any other distractions. We *act* in such a way that the
fear does not drive us to do something or stop us from
doing anything. Fear thrives on powerlessness, the belief

that we have no options. When we have a tool, such as the Triple A, we have an empowering alternative. Then we are less likely to be devastated by fear and it gradually becomes so ordinary that it loses its capacity to throw us off course.

7   *Openness to Feelings*

~ I am becoming more willing to express
all my own feelings and to receive those
of others, including fear, joy, grief, and
tenderness. I am practicing ways to show
anger nonviolently, in ways that are not
abusive, threatening, blaming, or out
of control.

Feelings are the built-in technologies with which nature
has endowed us to handle the givens of life: Since we will
experience loss, we have the ability to be sad and thereby
work through or resolve our grief. Since we will experience danger and threats, we have the ability to feel fear
and thereby go on the alert. Since we will experience injustice, we have the ability to become angry and thereby
right a wrong or at least show protest. We can make a
commitment to do this nonviolently, without hurting
others. We only let others know our feelings without
blaming them or demanding that they change to fit our
specifications. Likewise, we can learn a lot from watch-
ing others who show feelings in healthy ways. We can

open ourselves to the feelings that we arouse in others. We do this by simply listening. When the voice of ego inside us wants us to defend our position or deny our accountability, we do not speak our self-justification but rather continue listening. Such attention is a practice of mindfulness applied to communication.

8 *Respectful Assertiveness*

❧ I can become stronger in asking for what I want without demand, manipulation, or expectation. As I remain respectful of the timing, wishes, and limits of others, I can take no for an answer.

We can practice being assertive without being aggressive. This means that we ask for what we want but we do not force our will on others. We can hear a *no* and accept it, rather than pushing or harassing the other person. We can practice respect for the timing of others by not insisting that they take action as quickly as we would like. We accept the given that everyone operates on a unique timetable and our commitment is to the practice of patience and respect for this variety in human responsiveness. We can practice respect for the boundaries of others by not blaming them or attempting to force them to yield to our wishes. We can notice what others really want and not try to bamboozle them into doing things our way, even if we have the skill to do so. Aggression is the brand of control that makes our will more important than others' choices. Assertiveness is simultaneously rightful speech and respect for others' responses.

9   Not Taking Advantage

❧ I forgo taking advantage of anyone because of his ignorance, status, or financial straits. I forgo the chance to use any charms of word, body, or mind to seduce or trick others.

We may notice that we have an upper hand in some situations because we know more than the other person. We may also have more skill in persuasion, more power by reason of status or economic position. We may notice that someone is vulnerable because she is at a low ebb, depressed, or facing a crisis, including that of financial embarrassment. A person of character and spiritual standards will not take advantage of any of this. He will not go in for the kill but pull back and not exploit the situation. The practice is to act from a place of caring about others' plight, wanting to help them get back on their feet before we enter into transactions with them. We commit ourselves to look for an equal playing field. Most of us have skills we can use to trick or cheat others. Most of us can somehow seduce or convince others, perhaps against their will. Once we become more honest in all our dealings, we care more about being authentic than about what we can gain. If we are attractive to others just as we are, we are content. If we are unappealing or unconvincing, that is all right with us. Our goal is truth, not profitable consequences.

10   *Growing in Gratitude*

◦❧ I choose not to take unfair advantage of others' generosity. I am letting go of any sense of entitlement in favor of gratitude for whatever is given to me.

We can practice gratitude by beginning each day with a prayer or affirmation of thanks for all the people and circumstances in our lives that are contributing to our well-being. Many people find that they benefit from keeping a gratitude journal in which each day they write about three people or things that they are grateful for. We grow in integrity as we receive from others without taking too much from them. Their generosity might be over the top. We are watchful as to how others might deplete themselves to be of service to us. We show true caring as we insist they limit their giving especially when they cannot easily limit it themselves. We are not "takers." We let go of any sense of special entitlement. We realize as adults that we do not require others to take care of us; we take care of ourselves and others pitch in at times. We do the same for them. We make it a practice to give to those who give to us, not in an exact measure, but we do find ways to show our gratitude.

11   *Honoring Agreements and Boundaries*

❧ I try my best to keep my word, to honor
my commitments, and to follow through
on the tasks I agree to do. Accepting my
own limitations helps me to set sane limits
and boundaries with others. I no longer
make promises for the sake of pleasing or
appeasing others.

We respect ourselves more as we become people of our
word. If we agree to do something, we do it. Yet we make
it a practice to inquire into exactly what will be required
in any task or agreement and we ask ourselves if that re-
quirement fits us. We do not act out of obligation but out
of genuine willingness to help. We do not meet others'
demands because we want them to like us. The practice
of setting and maintaining personal boundaries includes:

- Acting cooperatively while being respectful of our
  own needs and plans
- Doing more for others only when doing so leads to
  helpful changes in their behavior or results that
  make a difference in their lives

- Contributing to a project but not doing all the work
- Seeking relationships that are reciprocal
- Acting based on explicit agreement and negotiation
- Offering help based on choice and not allowing ourselves to be guilt-tripped or manipulated into doing what we do not really want to do, especially by threats of abandonment
- Feeling that there is always a choice rather than being at the mercy or beck and call of the other
- Remaining guiltlessly able to say "no" or "enough" or "stop"
- Giving generously and reasonably and then letting go
- Assertively and kindly expressing to others what we feel, think, and want
- Handling money matters—loans, for example—with caution and objectivity

12 *Honest and True*

~❧ I am making sincere attempts to abide by
standards of rigorous honesty and truthfulness in all my dealings no matter how
others act toward me. My question is not
"What can I get away with?" but "What
is the right thing to do?" If I fall down in
this, I can admit it, make amends, and
resolve to act differently next time. Now
I more easily and willingly apologize when
necessary.

We can commit ourselves to acting honestly, fairly, and
generously in any dealings with others. We are not comfortable with any transaction that does not lead to both
ourselves and the other being satisfied with however the
deal is designed. We give up the tendency to cheat or to
get away with something. If we realize that we have
acted in dishonest ways, we can use the spiritual practices of admitting, making amends, and resolving to
change. Admitting our shortcomings and our misdeeds

is a powerful spiritual exercise since it involves recognizing how our actions impact others. In the twelve steps of recovery programs, step one involves admitting. Making amends, such as offering apologies and asking forgiveness, are spiritual practices since they place us in the unvarnished truth of our circumstances. They also demonstrate to ourselves and others that we are dedicated to changing. Transformation is a grace that may more likely come our way when we engage in practices like these. Our dedication opens us to a joy that now comes not simply from experiencing pleasure and comfort but from fearless integrity.

13   *Our Inventory*

~≈ I examine my conscience regularly. I am
   taking inventory not only of how I may
   have hurt others, but also of how I may not
   have activated or shared my gifts, how I
   may still be holding on to prejudices or the
   will to retaliate, how I may still not be as
   loving as I can be.

We can practice this commitment by taking a written inventory. In a journal, list the following:

1. The times we recall having hurt others intention-
   ally
2. The ways in which we have not utilized the gifts
   and talents we know we possess
3. The biases we hold within ourselves toward those
   we perceive to be different—whether or not we
   have acted on them
4. The times we did not show love or act in a loving
   way

After taking this inventory, we can promise, to ourselves and in the presence of one other person, to change our behavior in the future.

Next we can take a positive inventory of ourselves, listing the following:

1. How we have helped and loved others
2. Times when we have chosen to let go or reconcile rather than to seek revenge
3. Ways in which we are activating our gifts and potentials

We share this inventory as well with a friend or confidant, balancing our sense of our shortcomings with an acknowledgment of our virtues and strengths.

14 *No More Regrets*

~≈ As I struggle with regret or self-reproach
because of mistakes I have made in my life,
I am no longer ashamed of my fallibility.
I am more kind toward myself. I take all
my errors as learning experiences so I can
do better in the future. I make amends
wherever I can. My mistakes are becoming
a valuable passport to humility and to ten-
der compassion toward myself and others.

Sometimes, seemingly out of nowhere, a memory will
surface of a time we did not act in a loving or kind way
toward someone else, and we are filled with regret. When
this happens, we can send loving-kindness to that person. Such moments may be happening because that person somehow needs our love right then: a synchronicity
of need and resource. We can design our loving-kindness
practice with aspirations like these: "May I make up for
what I have done and be forgiven." "May you be happy
now so that whatever happened in the past no longer

harms you in any way." "May I be happy and forgiving now no matter how I was hurt in the past." "May we act lovingly and feel ourselves loved. May we feel and receive compassion. May we have equanimity no matter what is happening to us right now. May all beings have these same immeasurable joys." Now regret connects us to spiritual practice, rather than to a sense of shame. We can imagine that pilots of private airplanes probably spend 20 percent of their time staying on course and 80 percent correcting their course, and that they are content with those proportions!

15   *A Brighter Self-Image*

⤝ I am letting go of the need to keep up appearances or to project an impressive self-image. I notice that I am more willing to appear as I am, without pretense, and no matter how unflattering. As I settle into the reality of myself, with pride in my gifts and unabashed awareness of my limits, I notice that I more easily access happiness, sanity, and wisdom.

This commitment requires undertaking an honest assessment of our strengths and weaknesses. Here are some questions that may help us in this process:

How do I usually behave in my dealings with others?
What does my record show? Looking back to my family of origin, whose behavior or traits do I most imitate?
How do others see me?
What do others keep saying to me that I become defensive about?

What are my fantasies of what my life could be like?
What do I really want and what do I really cherish?
What are my fears and inhibitions?
What are my compulsions and addictions?
Am I mainly introverted or extraverted?
What are my prejudices?
How present am I when people are talking to me?

16 Just As We Are

～❧ I notice that my behavior and choices no
longer have to be quite so determined by
what others may think of me. I am giving
up any attempts to get others to accept or
love me. I do not change myself in order to
fit in. I am intent on portraying myself as I
am, no matter what the reaction of others.

We may notice that the opinions of others weigh heavily
upon us. Most of us carefully design a persona, a way of
appearing, that seems satisfactory to those whose opinion
matters to us. We may have begun constructing this false
self in childhood, especially if it was dangerous to be ourselves just as we were. As we accept ourselves more and
more, we value our unique qualities and know that we
have things to work on too. We can sit mindfully and
imagine that we are holding all our traits as if they were
tools. As we do so, we say yes to each of them as valuable
and as a device for learning and growing. Paradoxically,
such honesty is conducive to inner change and simultaneously releases us from being intimidated by others'

judgments. We become less afraid that others might see us in all our human fallibility, self-centeredness, and inadequacy. Paradoxically, this vulnerability actually makes us more appealing to others. In this practice, we are detaching the masks we were using to condition others' view of us. We let go of our ego-need to inflate ourselves, since our own unconditional truthfulness has become more exciting than praise.

> *I desire so to conduct the affairs of this administration that if, at the end, when I come to lay down the reins of power, I have lost every other friend on earth, I shall at least have one friend left, and that friend shall be down inside of me.*

—Abraham Lincoln

17 *Free Speech*

❧ I am less and less afraid of free speech—
my own or that of others. I am learning to
listen carefully to others' feedback rather
than to become defensive or ego-reactive
by it. I welcome feedback that shows me
where I am less caring than I can be, where
I am less tolerant, where I am less open.
When others call me on being inauthentic
or pretending, I am not defensive but
simply take it as information about what
I have to work on.

It may be difficult to receive feedback from others even
when it is meant to be helpful. Our ego may be overly
sensitive and on guard against anything that makes us
seem less than perfect. We can practice aspiring to an
openness to the truth about ourselves: "I keep opening
myself to whatever the truth about me may be. The more
I know myself, the more I can love myself and others
too." Likewise, we want to take stock of ourselves so we

can become more wise and loving. To accomplish this we look for feedback that might show us where our personalities can use some sprucing up. We welcome the comments of others rather than construing them all as insults or attacks. We practice this by becoming aware of how we defend against incoming information. We practice further by *asking* for feedback when we doubt the purity of our motivations or wonder about the impact of our behavior. "Did I come across harshly? If so, I want to soften my words, tone, or manner to be more respectful of you." Such self-disclosure is a practice of self-embarrassment, of willingness to appear awkward. These practices make us more faithful to ourselves and more appealing to others. Gradually, our self-esteem increases as we notice we care more about living truthfully than about being seen as perfect.

18   *Being Authentic*

~~ More and more, I blow the whistle on
myself when I notice myself being phony,
untruthful, passive-aggressive, or manipulative. I want to come clean right then and
there by admitting that I am acting falsely.
These are the ways I am choosing to be
more authentic in my relationships.

In addition to being open to feedback from others as a
way of finding out where our work is, we can also *police
ourselves*. The practice is to speak up and admit it the
minute we notice ourselves acting in ways that do not
present ourselves honestly. We simply pause and say
straight-out how we have just lied, been controlling, or
tried to make an impression that does not match who we
really are. For example, we might admit to someone,
"Don't be fooled by my manner. I'm acting as if I were
definite and on top of things when, in reality, I am full of
self-doubt." Here is an example of acknowledging a hidden motivation: "I'm asking if you want to go to the
movies not only because I enjoy your company, but

because I'm lonely." Such ruthlessly candid confession increases our humility and makes us less likely to be phony in the future. The embarrassment in this practice stings, and that conditions us to be more careful or authentic next time. Others will respect us for such frankness, but that is not our motivation. We do this to become more honest, not more admired.

19   *Seeing Ourselves*

~~~ When someone upsets me and it keeps
gnawing at me, I do not attribute it only
to the person and what he did. I take my
reaction as a signal that something has
been triggered in me, as a signal to look
at myself.

Be aware of any reaction that seems bigger than the
event warrants, any reaction that hangs on and eats away
at us. Perhaps it is pointing to something unnoticed and
feared within ourselves. We can do our best to S.E.E.
what is going on:

- Is this my *shadow*? Our shadow is the part of ourselves that we do not acknowledge or accept and
  tend to project onto others. We can ask if what has
  upset us is similar to our own hidden, disavowed,
  or unnoticed self and vow to acknowledge it.
- Is this my *ego*? Our ego can be so inflated that
  we are overly sensitive to others' reactions to us.
  We are aroused to fury or indignation when our

greatness is not honored, when our shortcomings are pointed out to us, when we are shown to be wrong, or when we are not granted full control. If so, we can notice those reactions and work with our wounded ego to calm down, accept our fallibility, and open up to what we can learn about ourselves.

• Is this my *early* life? Is this person or situation reminding me of pain or disappointments from my childhood? Our unfinished business from childhood may come to the fore when someone reminds us of how one of our parents treated us. We react to a person here and now based on feelings about our parent. This is called "transference." The work is to acknowledge transference when it arises. The first step is simply noticing it. Then we can work on healing the pain of our past in therapy or in whatever ways we have of exploring our "emotional baggage," so that we can finally live in the present. Living in the now is essential to love, realism, and acceptance.

20   *Dealing with Hurt*

〜 I do not knowingly hurt others. If others
  hurt me, I do not have to retaliate or punish them. Instead I open a dialogue and ask
  for amends. No matter what, I do not hate
  anyone or hold grudges.

We act lovingly in all our interactions with others because compassion is our practice. We make a vow not to
retaliate even in small ways. This does not mean letting
others walk all over us. It means resisting the immediate
impulse to pass on the hurt, the impulse to make others
feel as bad as we do. Instead, we choose to speak up when
others hurt us by reporting their impact on us, but not by
hurting them back. We show our anger directly and let
go of it rather than letting it turn into resentment or a
grudge. We do this by practicing healthy anger over and
over, even though our bruised ego advises us to hit back,
exact reprisals, make others pay. We are seeing ourselves
as people who have given up the primitive, gangland
style of revenge in favor of a threefold response: asserting
our reaction, not letting others continue to hurt us, and

looking for ways to bring about peace. Our commitment is to a creative style in human communication, one that finds an alternative to the same old retaliation. As part of this, we keep no record of wrongs. Hate is rage with an insatiable need to keep punishing and to keep exacting revenge. Some people feel ongoing hate, which is a sad and dangerous condition to be possessed by. As we become more spiritually evolved, we may feel *moments* of hate but we vow not to act them out and gradually they, and all the stress in their wake, subside.

> *May those whose hell it is*
> *To hate and hurt*
> *Be turned into lovers*
> *Bringing flowers.*
> —Shantideva

21 *Showing Kindness*

❧ I act kindly toward others not to impress or obligate them but because I really am kind—or working on it. If others fail to thank me or to return my kindness, that does not have to stop me from being loving nonetheless.

The practice of loving-kindness is not only a meditative practice but a lifestyle change. We commit ourselves to look for every way in which we can be kind to others in our words and deeds. Gradually, we will notice that we become kind even in our thoughts. This is a sign that the practice is working. Sometimes others turn on us or reject our offers of affection. There are three main options for us: we can continue to reach out, we can become angry and protest, or we can turn away from them in despair. The practice is to continue to reach out without trespassing on others' boundaries. This means that we can accept the fact that some people won't be responsive to our love. Loving-kindness then means that we wish them the best, we do not retaliate or punish, and we let go of making overtures but maintain the connection to them in our hearts. This is how the practice is a form of unconditional love, that is, a love not conditioned by whether it is returned or even acknowledged. To love in this way shows us we really can love purely, which is such good news. We can use the Buddhist practice of saying silently "May you experience happiness and the causes of happiness" to each person we encounter in one day.

22   *Not Giving Up on Others*

∼ I never give up on others. I believe that
everyone has an innate goodness and that
being loved can release it.

Not to give up in despair on the ultimate goodness in
others—no matter how they behave—means believing
that every person has an inherent, ineradicable goodness. Then we can trust that our love, even from afar, will
help bring it out into the open. This is a loving faith in
humanity, and one that releases more love into the
world. Some faith may seem like superstition or wishful
thinking. Yet operative faith in Buddha nature, Christ
consciousness, or the inner light of every human being is
an affirmation of our highest potential. When we activate this love in our behavior we are most richly ourselves. Our capacity to love and to believe in lovability is
not extinguished, nor does it have to be diminished by
what others do. We recall the words of Saint John of the
Cross: "Where there is no love, put love, then you will
find it."

Our practices are to

- look for goodness in others no matter what they say or do; no display gets in the way
- speak kindly to others in all circumstances
- notice any unkind thoughts and gently revise them into the language of loving-kindness
- act toward others with love no matter how they behave
- refuse to let others hurt or abuse us
- use the skillful means of nonviolence in response to aggression
- trust that our love will evoke the love that is waiting to open in their hearts

23 *Saying "Ouch!"*

~ I am becoming more able to say "ouch!" to
   pain and abuse in jobs, in relationships,
   and in any interactions with others. I want
   to take action to change what can be
   changed and to move on when situations
   remain abusive. I do this without self-pity
   or the need to make others wrong. When I
   stand up for my rights, I do not have to
   gloat if I am vindicated nor do I have to
   seek revenge if I am not.

In the practice of assertiveness we report the impact of
others' behavior on us directly to them. When they do
something that hurts us, we say "Ouch! and "No more of
that!" This is showing loving-kindness toward ourselves
and it alerts the other person as to how his behavior impacts people. Perhaps he did not realize that his actions
were causing pain. If he did realize it and wanted to inflict
pain, he needs to see that he cannot get away with it. The
interactions we have with others can thus be learning

experiences all around. To stand up for ourselves does not lead to gloating over our success nor should it be a subtle form of vengeance. We simply act in a straightforward way with a desire to communicate our pain and set our limits. This stabilizes and affirms us in the world of others. We then do not fall apart so easily when others come at us in hurtful ways. We have a commitment in place that combines four healthy responses: self-protection, not hurting others, stating our pain, and not staying in situations that prolong pain.

24   *How We Can Include*

~~ I notice that in some groups or communi-
ties, there are people who are put down,
demeaned, or excluded. Rather than be
comforted that I am still an insider, I sense
the pain of those who are outsiders. I can
reach out, speak up, and include everyone
in my circle of love.

Making the distinction between "insider" and "outsider"
is a common way we create a sense of safety for ourselves.
We are terrified about being outsiders, cut off from the
security of belonging to a group. A group of any kind is a
holding environment, one in which we can be ourselves
and feel accepted by others. We can also feel assured that
the group will protect us against outsiders. Yet the entire
distinction between inside and outside is a fiction. It has
no foundation in reality. In reality, we are one human
family. Insider versus outsider is an invention of the
primitive ego, still huddling around campfires for security
against a perilous world. We can be inclusive in any
group we are part of. We can decline membership in

groups that exclude. We can give up the primitive form of safety that insider groups offer in favor of the joy of reaching out to the human community without exception. We can imagine a circle with no distinct circumference and ourselves in the center drawing everyone into it. This poem can be our affirmation:

> He drew a circle that shut me out—
> Heretic, a rebel, a thing to flout.
> But Love and I had the wit to win:
> We drew a circle that took him in!
> —Edwin Markham, "Outwitted"

25   *Gossip-Free*

✎ I am avoiding gossip and the spreading of
rumors. Now, if I have something to say
about someone, I say it to him directly.

Gossip makes someone the last to hear what he has the
right to be the first to hear. Part of feeling that one is an
insider (as outlined in the previous commitment) is to
gossip about someone else, who then becomes the outsider. Our primitive need to be an insider in order to sur-
vive makes us feel warm and comfortable when we do
this. Part of becoming more spiritually aware is to give
up the primitive pleasures that so often create pain for
others, such as the pleasure we often take in successful
retaliation. Instead, we choose the joy of acting with
loving-kindness by not gossiping at all. If we do have
something to share, question, or report, we go to the
person directly and open a dialogue. This requires the
practice of assertiveness. Now we can see that a psychological tool such as assertiveness has a spiritual direction
in it, since it can be used in a way that makes us more
kind and loving. Addressing, processing, and resolving is

the alternative to gossip. We practice addressing when we bring up our issues with someone face-to-face. We practice processing when we share our feelings about and with that person. We practice resolving when we work things out so that there is greater understanding between us and no leftover resentment. The result is that there are no inside-outside distinctions, but only the one embrace we all so genuinely need.

26   *A Sense of Humor*

~≈ I have a sense of humor, but not at the
    expense of others. I am less and less apt
    to engage in ridicule, teasing, sarcasm, or
    the use of comebacks when others are
    sarcastic toward me. I seek simply to feel
    the pain in both of us and look for ways
    to bring more mutual respect into our
    communication.

Healthy humor pokes gentle fun at human foibles, especially our own. The negative side of humor is sarcasm,
ridicule, and prejudice. We may be engaging in these
and think it's all in fun. In reality, it is hurtful language,
the opposite of what Buddhists call right speech. We
can make a commitment not to engage in—or to listen
approvingly to—negative humor. We express our discomfort with jokes that show hate or bigotry. We can
notice the aggression in prejudice. We can notice the
pain-producing quality that lies beneath some of our
own or others' words. Our practice is to maintain cus-
tody over what we say so that we enjoy humorous

moments without having to humiliate anyone. We have then made loving-kindness more important in our lives than how entertaining we can be. Our practice is our best reward. We might also open a dialogue when someone is sarcastic toward us. Perhaps some aggression will then be lured from its dark hiding place in so-called humor and we can address it directly. Aggression is recognized as a favorite sport of ego and humor is often its weapon. As we invite kinder communication, words between us and others become more choiceful and less stinging. A new gentleness enters our relationships. We become more careful about hurting anyone, even unconsciously. "May I be free of aggression and detect every subtle form it takes."

27   *Facts, Not Flaws*

~⤳ More and more, I look at other people and
their choices without censure. I still notice
the shortcomings of others and of myself,
but now I am beginning to see them as
facts to deal with rather than flaws to be
criticized or be ashamed of. I do not laugh
at people's mistakes, distresses, or misfor-
tunes. I feel compassion and ask how I
can help.

Letting go of the tendency to judge others is not easy.
Our minds naturally assess people, places, and things. In-
telligent discernment can be distinguished from judgment, which happens when we censure, blame, or look
down on others for not adhering to rules we believe in.
That tendency is something we can work on through the
practice of mindfulness. Here is an example: We have a
friend whom we feel is overly controlling in her behavior
toward us. We sit with the reality of her behavior and
shave away our inclinations to editorialize, condemn, or

criticize it. We keep coming back to the pure reality of the other person in her basic goodness. We then open ourselves to compassion by our loving-kindness practice in which we say, "May she be released from the pain of having to be in control. May she realize she does not have to be controlling and thereby find her true spiritual powers. May I too realize I do not have to judge others but can assess and bless. May all people discover the enlightened path of loving-kindness."

28   *Critics No More*

❦ I avoid *criticizing, interfering,* or giving *advice*
that is not specifically asked for. I take
care of myself by staying away from those
who use this "C.I.A." approach toward me.

We can affirm here and now that we will beware of our
natural tendency to criticize others, interfere in their af-
fairs, or give advice that is not specifically requested of
us. This applies especially to our conversations with family members and those with whom we are in an intimate
relationship. We imagine that we are being of help but it
may be that we rush to the C.I.A. responses because we
are not yet comfortable *simply being with* others in their
pain or predicaments. Thus, the second part of the practice is to remain present to those who tell us of their
problems, with no attempts to fix or editorialize. We are
present when we manifest the five A's in our listening
style: attention, acceptance, appreciation, affection, and
allowing him to have his own feelings in his own time
and way. These A's are the opposites of criticizing, interfering, and advising. The five A's are indeed the tools by

which we can bring out the best in others. We might at first feel afraid that we are not doing much good when we simply sit and listen with the five A's, but it will soon be obvious that such real presence creates the intimacy of trust, a healing container for someone's pain. Were we engaging in C.I.A. because we feared such intimacy all along? We can practice looking into our motivations as much as we practice upgrading them.

29   Being Consistent

❧ I am focusing on becoming consistent:
being the same kind of person at home,
at work, in my friendships, and in all my
day-to-day dealings. I choose to show
equal respect and sincerity toward
strangers as I show toward those close
to me and vice versa.

Some of us notice we are angels with strangers and
demons with those we are close to. It is natural to be so
secure with our family members or with our partners that
we become uninhibited. We then may not show the same
respect toward them as we do so automatically to people
at work or in other outside circumstances. Home becomes the place where we feel we should have free rein,
where we exercise no limit over our words or actions. The
healing practice has three parts: We can notice this and
ask for feedback about it from those we live with. We can
pledge to them that we will act respectfully. We can ask
them to call us on our shortcomings in this regard. On the
other hand, we might act kindly to those close to us and

be unkind, brusque, or rude toward strangers. Our three practices then are: We apologize if we treat someone curtly. We make it a point to show respect to strangers. We go out of our way to be courteous to others, especially other drivers or those who serve us in stores, restaurants, and so forth. This is how we manifest our loving-kindness everywhere rather than simply wishing it for everyone.

30   *Cherishing What Matters*

❧ I am thankful for the set of values that I
   received in the course of my life from
   so many sources. At the same time, I am
   examining the scaffolding of beliefs, biases,
   assumptions, and myths that I inherited
   from family, school, religion, and society.
   One by one, I seek to dismantle and
   discard those values not in keeping with
   loving-kindness and emotional maturity
   and to cherish those that are.

We cherish the values that we have lived by. We look
carefully at the beliefs that flow from these values. What
are the assumptions about human nature upon which
they rest? What are the values from our past that still
make sense? The practice is in the examination of all
that we have believed so that we can clean house—the
inner house of the mind that waits to be updated and that
wants to be free. We can look into our belief system and
the myths that drive our lives. We can ask which ones

still fit and which ones are ready to be dispensed with, since they alienate us from others. This is not giving in to the contemporary world that seems to have fewer firm values, but rather honing the values we have so that they fit better with who we are now and who everyone else has become. We can be people of conviction but we do not have to be rigid. We can widen our mental view so that we let in new beliefs and gain a more expansive way of seeing the world and of how we can be fully alive in it.

31 *Welcoming Lifestyles*

༄ I have a lifestyle of which I can be proud
and with which I can be content. My
family and friends may have lifestyles
different from mine. I do not look down
on them nor do I refuse to participate in
the conventional social rituals that make
them happy.

We value our own lifestyle and are open about it, with
no sense of shame. We honor the lifestyles of others, no
matter how different from our own. Abraham Maslow
studied self-actualized people and reported: "The self-actualized person will go through the rituals of convention
with a good-humored shrug and the best possible grace."
That shrug is a spiritual act since it shows compassion
for others and openness on our part to the diversity of
human experience. It does not harm us nor does it di-
minish our own individuality to participate in harmless
rituals that mean a lot to others, for instance, calling
home on holidays, coming to Thanksgiving dinner, or
showing up in times of illness or death in the family. Our

ego has to be put on report if it does not permit us to show this kind of respect to others, especially those of a former generation. We can make it a point to act with graciousness toward the customs others cherish. As we do this, we become bigger at heart. We then grow in self-esteem and are loved more by those who notice our generosity.

32   *The Real Success*

~& I can now measure my success by how
much steadfast love I have, not by how
much money I have in the bank, how much
I achieve in business, or how much power I
have over others. Expressing my full and
unique capacity to love is becoming the
central focus of my life.

Our values become more spiritually sound as we focus
on showing love rather than on gaining control over
others. Each of us has a unique handwriting, a unique
ability in art, a unique way of working. We can become
enormously interested in what our artful working signa-
ture of love might look like, the specific brand of love
that is in us. This search leads to our stretching ourselves to go the extra mile in how we show love, to go to
greater lengths in our generosity, to love beyond our immediate circle of friendships into the wider world. Our
commitment is to make this practice of stretching our

ways of loving as important as regular physical stretching and exercise. This daily, hourly vow may help:

May I show all the love I have
In every way I can
To everyone I meet
In every here and now.

33   *Awareness of Influences*

~≪ I am less and less under the blinding influ-
ence of the three main streets that direct
so many attitudes and lifestyles: Madison
Avenue, Wall Street, and Hollywood
Boulevard.

As we work toward becoming more loving and mature
human beings, we become wary of the media and the ad-
vertising industry, of Madison Avenue, which seeks to
make us want more all the time. We choose not to be
driven by Wall Street's greed for more and more money,
whether or not we really need it. We commit ourselves to
not being so influenced by Hollywood that we might
doubt the value of our ordinary existence, which lacks
the glamour, muscle, and perfection that we see on the
movie screen. We also do not seek the romantic dramas
we see in movies and television but choose the challenges and comforts of authentic, real-world love.

Moving away from these three streets, we choose instead to stand on the corner of Mindfulness and Loving-

Kindness. There we are dressed as we choose, not compelled to sport the latest fashion unless we genuinely like it. From that corner we love sanely and can see everyone else without envy. We arrived there on foot or driving the vehicle that serves our needs, rather than the one that makes the biggest impression. There are no movies there, only the moving reality of who we are in all our contented ordinariness.

34 *No Longer Fooled*

✎ I am learning not to be swayed by opportunities for quick gain, by sweet talk or rhetoric, or by any other seductions that might lead me to transgress my boundaries or to act foolishly or immorally. I cherish the joy of a good conscience more than what I may gain or what I can get away with.

Like Pinocchio, we are sometimes at the mercy of the tricksters who have predatory skill in the arts of persuading us to act against our better judgment. The chance to make a bundle or to get ahead quickly may make us lose touch with our own convictions. As we grow in spiritual consciousness we notice the power in gain, greed, or illusion. We also notice how we can talk ourselves into misconduct. We ask for strength to fight off the voices of promise and not to let ourselves become prey to them. We decide to act in accord with the highest standards no matter what the benefit we might thereby miss out on. We choose to maintain a clear conscience. That matters more than how we put one over on someone, how we got off scot-free, or made a fortune. All that matters to us is that we acted with self-respect, something much more valuable than whether we make a killing or stay on top. The top comes to look like the heaven of a communion of humanity, our best position to show love, rather than the summit from which we can look down on others or chuckle over having more than they.

35 *Sources of Bliss*

∼ I am enthusiastically seeking, or have
found, meaningful work and projects,
and these are the source of my bliss. I keep
discovering my deepest needs, wishes,
values, and potentials and living more and
more in accord with them.

It is ideal to be in a job that gives us a sense of accom-
plishment and contribution. Not all of us have that priv-
ilege, and so we can look at our work life and ask where
we go from here. We maintain our belief in the possibility of change by seeking the work we truly enjoy. At the
same time, we can be realistic about our hopes. We can
explore our deepest needs, values, and wishes and ask if
they have become lost in the shuffle of making a living.
If we cannot find work that feeds our soul, we can have a
hobby, a project, or an avocation that does. To locate our
inner needs, we can use this checklist:

What has consistently brought me happiness and a
sense of fulfillment?

What in my life arises from choice and what from obligation?

Does my daily routine and lifestyle match my present goals? For example, if my goals are meaningful work and enjoyment of friends, then my present routine may be just right even though I may have fantasies of flying off somewhere. If my goals are rugged physical challenges and hair-raising adventure, then climbing Mount Everest is a better fit than staying at home.

How would my life be different if my fantasies and ideals were fulfilled?

What do I admire in others?

What would I like to see happen for those I love? (This is often a clue to what we want for ourselves.)

What are my fears of risk in breaking out of the box?

What is being communicated to me through meaningful coincidences and dreams?

36   *Pride in Accomplishments*

∼≈ I have reason to be proud of some accomplishments. Thoreau wrote in his journal:
   "A man looks with pride at his woodpile." I
   see my commitments to integrity and love
   as my "woodpile."

It is a boost to our self-esteem to give ourselves credit for
our accomplishments and to receive graciously the admiration or compliments of others about our successes. We
look at our life story and realize we have done some important things. We can look at them now as if they were
a woodpile neatly cut and stacked by us. We can commit
ourselves to the practices in this book and the result is
that our sense of our success and our self-esteem increase.
We appreciate our gifts and how we have opened and
shared them. We notice our limitations and honor them,
while at the same time we keep looking for ways to transcend them. We know it is never too late to begin and it
is always too early to give up.

37 *Life Purpose*

❧ I ask this question as I embark upon any
relationship or project: Is this a suitable
context for me to fulfill my life purpose?
My life purpose is to live out the unique
and exuberant potential that is in me, to
love with all my might, and to share my
personal gifts in any way and everywhere
I can.

We audit our life projects and relationships. We do this
by regularly asking questions like these and making any
change, however small, that respects our answers:

Am I happy in this?
Do I feel threatened, scared, or disrespected?
Am I accepted as I am and encouraged to act in
accord with my own deepest needs, values, and
wishes?
Do I feel the five A's coming my way: attention,
acceptance, appreciation, affection, and allowing?

How do I take action today to begin to address what needs to be worked on and thereby resolved?

Do I see colleagues, friends, and relatives as partners or as competitors?

Am I a partner and team player or do I insist on dominating or on letting myself be dominated?

Am I activating my unique potential to love?

Am I open to others' love for me?

38   *Freedom from Stress*

∼≪ I am willing to work hard to fulfill my life
purpose but not to sacrifice my health by
seeking to please others or gain status,
fame, or fortune (the central values of the
chronically uneasy ego). The primary focus
of my life has become being a good person.

Consider this statement by James Fox, abbot of the Trap-
pist monastery at Gethsemane, about his own spiritual
journey:

> I found myself asking, *Is this what life is for, to
> burn it up in sweating, steaming, and toiling in a
> race for power, prestige, passion, pleasure, and piles
> of stocks and bonds, from every one of which I am
> going to be separated some day?*

Here are some useful questions for contemplating our
priorities, motivations, and stress levels:

> Am I always exhausted when I come home from
> work?

Is my work schedule impacting my health and
    well-being?
Am I trying to maintain a lifestyle that is beyond
    my means?
Have I bitten off more than I can chew in my
    attempt to maintain a certain status?
Is my mind taken up all day with work so that I
    rarely find time to eat properly, relax adequately,
    or sleep long enough?
Are my addictions increasing?
Are my worries mounting?
Is what exhausts me more than can be cured by a
    night's sleep?

Based on my responses to the questions above, what
actions should I take?

39 *Taking Our Turn*

❧ I am choosing not to push others aside so
that I can get ahead. I choose neither to
exalt myself nor to abase myself. Instead, I
take my turn, without complaint, at being
first, last, or midway in the long series of
lineups that life has in store for all of us.

One of the sternest givens of life is that we don't always
come in first. This may be difficult for the arrogant or entitled ego to handle. Humility means accepting our place
in line even though we may believe we deserve to get
ahead of others. Patiently standing in line in a store is a
simple and helpful practice in this area. We do not push
others aside; rather we honor their place and insist they
honor ours. We thereby combine respect for others' rights
with protection of our own boundaries.

In addition, we no longer try to get ahead by hoping
that others fail. We are unwilling to accept advances at
work, for instance, if it means making others lose their
jobs. At the same time, it is always legitimate to work
hard to get ahead, to increase our skills so we will be

recognized and advanced. We compete with our own record, another way to grow in self-esteem. The spiritual practice of saying yes to the lineups we encounter in life does not mean we do not compete at all, only that we do not do so in a cutthroat way. Our respect for ourselves allows us to get ahead; our caring for others does not let us step on them to get there.

Enlightenment means having no rank.
—Lin-chi, Chinese Buddhist teacher

40   *Less Competition*

> ~✎ I am less and less competitive in relation-
> ships and find an uplifting joy in coopera-
> tion and community. I shun situations in
> which my winning means that others have
> to lose in a demeaning way.

Healthy people want everyone to win. Competitiveness,
especially in intimate bonds, fortifies our ego rather than
our relationships. People respond to us more affection-
ately when we show ourselves to be cooperative. Com-
petition can be a way of avoiding that intimacy. The
practice consists simply of looking for ways to join with
others rather than to compete with them. We work
things out together so that both sides feel heard and both
sides gain. Such mutuality leads us also no longer to pit
one friend or partner against another. Nor do we try to
make a partner jealous of us. We look for ways to act in
accord with a mutuality model instead of a domination
model. We shun participation in business enterprises
that ensure a profit for us while impoverishing others.
Even in sports, we can become interested in how the

other players can play better more than in how we can trounce them. Behind these practices is a realization that our life goal is not top dog over underdog but equality in victory. Our calling is then to help one another, and, if we cannot help others, at least we commit ourselves to not harming them.

41   *Egoless Intimacy*

꙳ In intimate relationships, I put effort into
honoring equality, keeping agreements,
working through problems, and being
truly affectionate. My goal is not to use
my relationship to gratify my ego but to
dispossess myself of ego to gratify the
relationship.

Reacting defensively from ego is a major obstacle to an
intimate relationship. The practice of letting go of ego
means letting go of the arrogant or inflated belief in our
own primacy at the expense of others. The neurotic ego
is the F.A.C.E. we are always wanting to save: *fear* of not
being liked and honored, *attachment* to being right, *control* of others and of situations, and *entitlement* to be loved
and respected unconditionally with no reciprocal obligation. These are all compulsions that become forms of
pain for us and for those who have to deal with us. The
practice is to question our reactions to others, to tick
down the list, F.A.C.E., to check in with exactly how our
ego has been aroused. Then we make a commitment to

reversing the ego traits on our list: Fear becomes love. Attachment becomes letting-go. Control becomes allowing. Entitlement becomes standing up for ourselves but not over others.

Sitting quietly by ourselves, we take a few deep breaths and say, "Where I am afraid, let me love. Where I am attached, let me let go. Where I am trying to be in control, let me allow others to be who they are and in any situation may I let the chips fall where they may. Where I feel entitled, let me stand up for my reasonable rights and not retaliate if I cannot secure them now."

42   *Healthy Sexuality*

❧ More and more, my sexuality expresses
love, joyful playfulness, and responsibility.
I am letting go of any guilt and phobia
from childhood in favor of an adult style
of relating and enjoying.

Thomas Merton defines purity in a way that may not reflect what we were taught in childhood: "It is precisely
in the spirit of celebration, gratitude, and joy that true
purity is found." It is an adult spiritual practice to honor
our sexuality by relocating it in enjoyment and in responsibility. This may mean taking a careful inventory
of our sexual behavior: We explore the places in our
sexuality that may still be held hostage by puritanical
beliefs meant to scare rather than liberate us. For instance, we may believe that it is wrong to seek sexual
pleasure as an end in itself or that erotic fantasy is ver-
boten if it extends beyond conventional limits. We notice if in our sexual style we exploit or take advantage of
others. We notice if we are using sex as a weapon or in
any other manipulative way. We notice if our authentic

sexual orientation is still hidden or is now opening more courageously. We notice if our sexual style has become addictive in any way. If so, we begin changing this. Finally, we wonder if we believe that sex does not fit into spirituality, that is, that our whole self does not fit into spirituality. We can make a commitment to bring consciousness of our sexuality into our most sacred moments as a way of letting the spirituality of sex be acknowledged. William Blake wrote: "The Lamb of God sports in the gardens of sexual delight."

43 *Caution about Addiction*

∼ I am learning to keep better tabs on my use of food, alcohol, drugs, sex, gambling, and shopping, knowing they can be vehicles of addiction. I am always looking for ways to show moderation without self-inhibition.

Most of us are afflicted with an addiction of some kind. Addiction means dependency on something outside ourselves to get us through life's challenges, to celebrate successes, or to help us avoid reality, especially when it becomes uncomfortable. We might not even notice how we do this. It takes careful looking, willingness to admit what we are up to, and freedom from denial to see how addicted we may have become. The best pathway is that of checking in with others who know us. They can usually see our addictions better than we can: "Does my drinking seem over the top to you?" If the response we get is "yes" and we fight it tooth and nail, or if we become strongly annoyed when others show concern about our drinking without being asked, we definitely have something to look at. Recovery from an addiction requires a spiritual program. The 12-step programs fit the bill and introduce us to a set of practices that really work. We might balk at programs like this. The reason behind our resistance to repair may be in the fact that an addiction has a life of its own, one it wants to preserve; so, for instance, we won't want to keep going back to Alcoholics Anonymous *because* it really works. That is the challenge that takes true perseverance and openness to the ardent grace that wants us to be whole.

44 Body Consciousness

◦ I am more conscious of my body and
its well-being. I am adjusting my diet,
exercise, and health habits to care for
myself responsibly.

We can take positive action to become more healthy. We
can adjust our diets in keeping with what is good for us.
We can engage in regular exercise and avoid harmful en-
vironments and behaviors. Such concern about physical
health is a spiritual concern, since only as healthy people
can we fulfill our life's purpose of personal fulfillment and
sharing our gifts. We tend to separate our physical, emotional, psychological, sexual, and spiritual needs. In reality, they work together or not at all. Nowadays we are
blessed with great resources of information on how that
can happen. At the same time, we are bombarded with
information on how to avoid looking our age, how to
reduce wrinkles, how to lift our body parts away from
gravity, and so on. We can remain fit while not falling
prey to promises of cosmetic immortality. We can love

the changing looks the years depict in us. We can reconcile ourselves to our own bodies as a path to peace, as Thich Nhat Hanh wisely recommends. Then true health is a yes to the given of changes and endings.

45   *Confronted with a Suffering World*

➤ I am aware of the pain and poverty of those
less fortunate than myself. Confronted
with the suffering in the world, I do not
turn my eyes away nor do I get stuck in
blaming God or humanity, but simply ask,
"What then shall *I* do?" I keep finding
ways to respond with time, attention,
money, and myself, no matter how mini-
mal: "It is better to light one candle than to
curse the darkness."

As we arouse in ourselves a feeling of warmth for those
who suffer, we let ourselves be touched by suffering in the
wider world, not only in our own circle of loved ones.
This is how we cross over our narrow boundaries so love
can be universal in and through us. We then look for specific ways to be of help. It is not enough to feel compassion; we do best to show it in action. Not all of us are
called to leave our life routine or our daily responsibilities
behind in order to go to faraway places as aid workers. We

are not less valuable to the world because we stay at home and make a donation to a cause or write our congressperson about one. The point is to let our compassion and concern activate us. In great compassion, our caring about suffering means a commitment to relieve it: "May you be free of suffering" then becomes "I commit myself to help that happen." The challenge is to find some form of implementation of our inner feeling of caring.

46   *Political Awareness*

꙳ My work on myself is making me more
   conscious of political issues in today's
   world. I am learning to question authority.
   I am looking for ways to work for an end to
   war, retaliation, greed, hate, and ignorance. I have not given up on believing in
   the possibility of a transformation of the
   world and of every political and religious
   leader.

A spiritual orientation includes hope in the possibility of
the spiritual evolution of every political or religious
leader. We don't give up on them. We may strongly dis-
agree with a president's policies. When we see him on
TV, we may immediately feel anger or we may judge him
as lacking in intelligence or integrity. It is a spiritual practice to change that reaction by saying, aloud or silently,
every time we see him: "May you become a pioneer of
peace. May you develop wisdom and compassion." These
aspirations do not take the place of informing ourselves

about political issues, questioning authority, taking a stand against policies we see as immoral, or engaging in protest. Hope for world peace or world change or the transformation of leaders is not a wish. It is a powerful respect for basic human goodness and the potential of transformation in the world. Hope is hope in grace.

47   Dedication to Nonviolence

❧ I am committing myself to resisting evil
and fighting injustice in nonviolent ways.
This is how I focus on restorative justice,
not retributive justice.

Columbia University professor Robert Thurman writes,
"If one sincerely upholds the truth, its simple power will
eventually overwhelm injustice." Do we believe that? If
we do, we won't give up, neglect to take a stand, or believe our individual efforts "make no difference." We will
trust the power in our voice to contribute to a critical
mass of commitment to nonviolence so that a change
can happen in world politics. We are not naive enough
to deny the workings and the endurance of the collective
shadow. We know that there will always be violence of
some kind in the world. Yet we trust that there will also
always be hands raised not in aggression but in protest
against violence and in cheer for the ways of peace. We
become more spiritually aware as we see ourselves never
giving up on the possibility of more love on the world
stage and the possibility of acting in ways to make that

happen during our lifetime. *There will never be only love or only peace, but there can be more love than before we got here and more peace because we stayed here.*

48   *Holding the Globe*

❧ I am distressed and feel myself called to
action by the disasters of pollution, global
warming, economic injustice, racial op-
pression, nuclear armaments, and viola-
tions of human rights. I keep thinking
globally and acting locally in any way
I can.

Our spirituality creates an immediate bond between
noticing injustice and taking action to deal with it. We
do this, as always, within the limits of our own resources
and in accord with the nature of our personal calling. Yet
every one of us can do something, even if it is simply re-
cycling and voting. Our practice is local and individual
while our consciousness remains universal. It may also be
helpful to design a spiritual practice in response to hearing the daily news. We do not simply listen to a broadcast
or watch a television transmission of the horrors that
happen daily; we do so with a sense of grief, compassion,
and mission. Then the communication of news is spiritually interactive. We feel sad, angry, and afraid for the

losses and terrors. We show our compassion for those who suffer by our prayer or aspiration in the moment of hearing the news. And our mission will be to respond in any way that is appropriate to our circumstances.

49   Love of Nature

❧ My love of nature makes me tread
   gently on the earth with what Saint
   Bonaventure called "a courtesy toward
   natural things."

Nature is the center of all aliveness. We humans are stewards of nature not owners of it. We are part of nature not rulers of it. We show our consciousness of this when we treat natural things with respect. Our commitment to cherish and preserve nature means that we do not destroy nor do we support companies that destroy natural habitats for the sake of monetary gain or the extension of our own comforts. We take a stand against every corporate interest that subjects nature to danger in order to increase its profit. We do not invest in companies that cause harm to the environment. These days we are in possession of so much information about how our lifestyle affects the balance of nature. When we do our homework and follow it up with support for those who protect the environment, we are taking action as citizens of the universe and we are on track spiritually too, since spiritual consciousness is truly universal.

The person who is nature-oriented is not only the one who seeks the hospitality of the woods, but the one who grants hospitality to all people. You are as prone to love as the sun is to shine; it being the most delightful and natural employment of the soul.... For certainly he that delights not in love makes vain the universe.... The whole world ministers to you as the theatre of your love.

—Thomas Traherne, seventeenth-century
    Anglican mystic

50   *Our Ideals*

～❧ I admire certain people, alive or dead, who
represent the ideals I cherish. I see them
not as idols but as models of what I can accomplish and mirrors of my own potential.

We can associate ourselves with a teacher who helps us
in our spiritual development. A trustworthy teacher is
one who transmits a truth, acts as a model of it, and keeps
showing us how we can become who we truly are (rather
than insisting we keep coming back to him to get what
only he has). A true teacher helps us leave him.

We can commit ourselves to learning from a teacher,
remaining aware that the teachings themselves are our
teacher—he or she is only a mouthpiece. Second, it is
important to look at *how* we admire teachers whom we
know and teachers whom we admire from afar, such
as the Dalai Lama, or from the past, such as Mother
Theresa. If we see them as absolutely perfect, we may be
caught in childish idolizing or in denial of the human
shadow. Our practice is to experience adult admiration:
We respect our heroes while knowing they have failings.

We remind ourselves that they are human after all. Then our ideals stay connected to what it means to be human.

A healthy ideal is not perfection but a close approximation of being a true human. Our role models will have powers and virtues, failings and defects, and a commitment to self-correction. Mostly, a true teacher will have a habit of returning every bow to him with one that points at us.

51   *Spiritual Power*

⤺ I see my own love and wisdom as gifts,
spiritual energies that do not come from
me but act through me. I say thanks for
these encouraging graces and yes to the
stirring call to live up to them.

Spirituality is not achieved by effort; it is received by
grace, the free gift of special help on the path to transformation. Our efforts certainly place us in the best position
for grace to come our way. We can put great effort into
changing ourselves and the world. Only grace can evince
the shifts that make the final difference. Grace is not
outside us; it is deep within our souls awaiting release. It
is the extra burst of wisdom and courage from our inner
goodness that makes us transcend our own limits. A yes
to powers beyond ego and gratitude for the graces that we
receive helps release more graces into the world through
us. The self-help movement sometimes emphasizes how
we can create our own reality. This can deteriorate into
the illusion that the ego has full control. It disregards the
power of unconscious forces, especially those of dreams,

synchronicity, the shadow, divine powers, and grace. As we progress in spiritual awareness, we pay attention to all these forces in and around us. We become deeply thankful for how graciously they keep coming to help us. Then we more clearly notice the vast number of our spiritual resources and guides. Carl Jung wrote: "Attention to the unconscious pays it a compliment that guarantees its cooperation."

52   *Placing Our Intention*

〜 Though I am not always successful in virtuous living or upholding my commitments, these are the ideals I am shooting for, the values I am placing an intention to live by.

The commitments presented in this book are recommendations. Each of us has to live them in ways that are compatible with our own unique gifts and circumstances. They need not become yet another reason to feel guilty or inadequate. Ideals are meant to be striven for, not ever fully achieved. We do all we can. We strive to place ourselves in the best position to grow psychologically and spiritually. Though we put in effort, at times, we do not accomplish what we planned; at times we slack off or procrastinate. All that matters is that we start over one more time than we give up, get cracking one more time than we pull back, keep going back to the drawing board one more time than we abandon it. Success with these commitments lies not in perfect compliance but in frequent return. It is never too late to come back to our practices, which is yet another way to summon hope.

Conclusion

To prevent unfavorable circumstances and adversity
from afflicting your mind ... put a stop to aversion
toward inner and outer obstacles. ... Practice seeing
everything in a solely agreeable way. For that to
happen, stop seeing harmful situations as something
wrong, but give all your effort to seeing them as valuable.

—Jigme Tenpey Nyima

The human heart is surely a most precious and mysterious reality. It can be strong and yet it can be hurt. It can open and yet it can close. It can include others in love and yet it can exclude others because of fear. Such polarities need not discourage us. Instead, they can point us to our splendid evolutionary task: We humans are here to go beyond fear and limitation so we can become ever more open to love. Indeed, we were given a lifetime just for that.

The hurts and harms we meet along the path of life can make us close up but, at the same time, they can be just what we need to open or reopen. This is how the world, and our predicaments in it, cooperate in helping us evolve. The commitments in this book are our way of cooperating with such evolutionary forces.

Goodness is always here inside us and always everywhere around us. An emphasis on commitments can give the impression that action is all it takes to express it. Yet, we do not have to *make* goodness come through, only *let* it through. It wants to show itself over and over.

I still believe, even after all the dark events of recent history, that we humans can trust that deep down we are a most pure goodness, consciousness, and bliss. We do not have to search for all this light, but only commit ourselves to integrity and loving-kindness and it will beam through us and through everything that happens to us. Then we can share it with unwearying gentleness among all our fellow pilgrims. No, it does not take long to notice the good news that light is our true nature and that love is how we show it.

Join me in this final thought: We are part of the birth of a new humanity, delivered from the womb of the ego-encapsulated world. The cries we hear are pangs of birth. And the planetary smile of the new little being looking at Mother Earth is happening now.

We cannot rest till everyone mirrors
the divinity in everything.

—Hermann Graf Keyserling

About the Author

David Richo, PHD, MFT, is a psychotherapist and workshop leader who lives in Santa Barbara and San Francisco, California. He combines Jungian, transpersonal, and mythic perspectives in his work. He is the author of:

*The Power of Coincidence: How Life Shows Us What We
  Need to Know* (Shambhala, 2007)

*Mary Within Us: A Jungian Contemplation of Her Titles
  and Powers* (Human Development Books, 2007)

*The Sacred Heart of the World: Restoring Mystical Devotion
  to Our Spiritual Life* (Paulist Press, 2007)

*The Five Things We Cannot Change: And the Happiness
  We Find by Embracing Them* (Shambhala, 2005)

*How to Be an Adult in Relationships: The Five Keys to
  Mindful Loving* (Shambhala, 2001)

*Catholic Means Universal: Integrating Spirituality and
  Religion* (Crossroad, 2000)

*Shadow Dance: Liberating the Power and Creativity of
  Your Dark Side* (Shambhala, 1999)

*When Love Meets Fear: How To Become Defense-Less
  and Resource-Full* (Paulist Press, 1997)

How to Be an Adult: A Handbook on Psychological and Spiritual Integration (Paulist Press, 1991)

For more information, including upcoming events and a catalogue of audio programs, visit davericho.com.